# My State
# NORTH CAROLINA

By Christina Earley



## TABLE OF CONTENTS



A Crabtree Seedlings Book

Crabtree Publishing
crabtreebooks.com

# School-to-Home Support for Caregivers and Teachers

This book helps children grow by letting them practice reading. Here are a few guiding questions to help the reader build his or her comprehension skills. Possible answers appear in red.

## Before Reading:

- What do I know about North Carolina?
    - *I know that North Carolina is a state.*
    - *I know that North Carolina has mountains.*
- What do I want to learn about North Carolina?
    - *I want to learn which famous people were born in North Carolina.*
    - *I want to learn what the state flag looks like.*

## During Reading:

- What have I learned so far?
    - *I have learned that Raleigh is the state capital of North Carolina.*
    - *I have learned that the Blue Ridge Parkway is 469 miles (755 km) long.*
- I wonder why...
    - *I wonder why the state flower is the flowering dogwood.*
    - *I wonder why North Carolina grows so many sweet potatoes.*

## After Reading:

- What did I learn about North Carolina?
    - *I have learned that you can watch kayaking at the U.S. National Whitewater Center.*
    - *I have learned that the state animal is the Eastern gray squirrel.*
- Read the book again and look for the glossary words.
    - *I see the word **capital** on page 6, and the word **parkway** on page 15. The other glossary words are found on pages 22 and 23.*

NORTH CAROLINA
Hi! My name is Alexis. Welcome to North Carolina!

I live in Asheville. There are mountains around my city.

There are more than 250 waterfalls near Asheville!

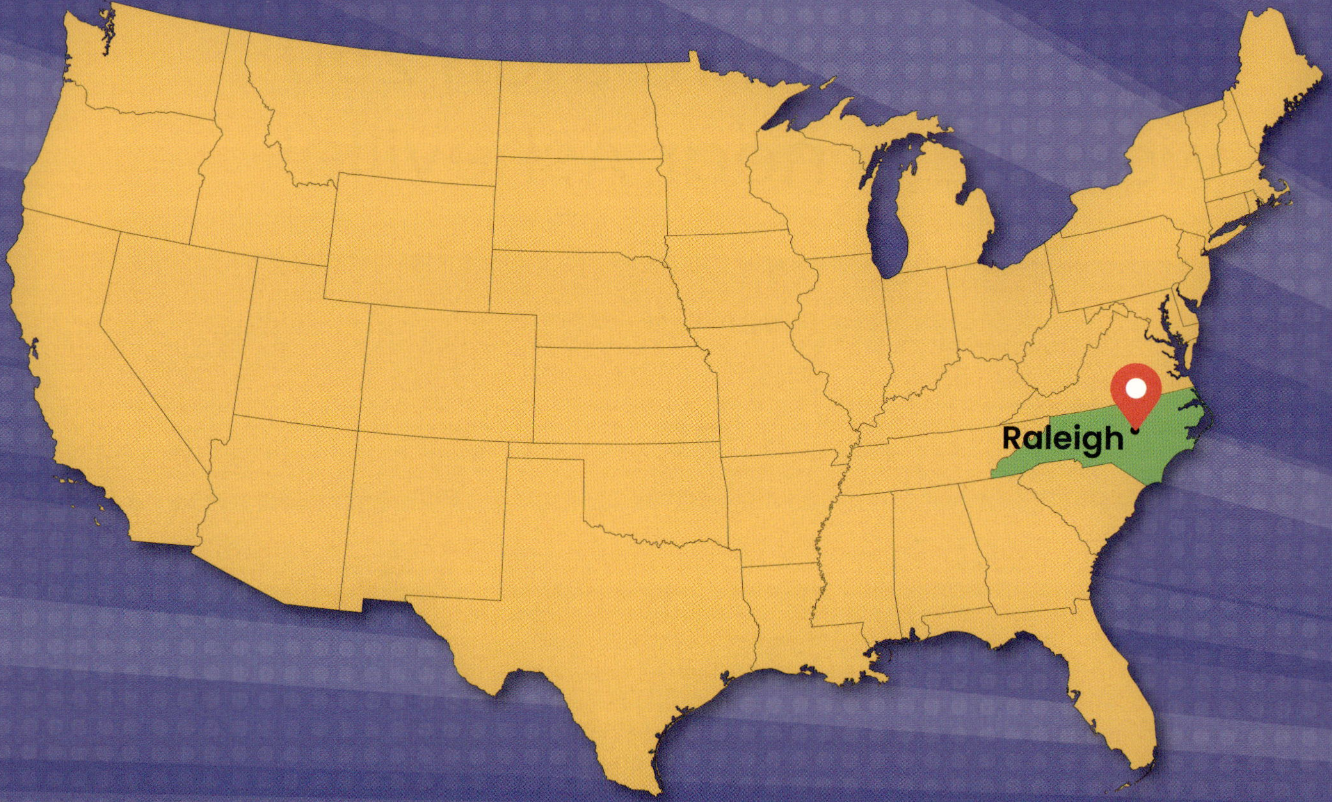


North Carolina is in the southeastern United States. The **capital** is Raleigh.

Fun Fact: Charlotte is the largest city in North Carolina.

The state animal is the Eastern gray squirrel.

The flowering **dogwood** is the state flower.

We grow a lot of **sweet potatoes**. Some of them are used to make sweet potato pie—my favorite!

Fun Fact: North Carolina grows more sweet potatoes than any other state in the U.S.

My state flag has a red, white, and blue stripe. It has a white star on the left.

There are three national sports teams in North Carolina.

My family likes to go for drives on the Blue Ridge **Parkway**. Sometimes we see black bears.

Fun Fact: The Blue Ridge Parkway is 469 miles (755 km) long.

I go fishing on the beaches of the Outer Banks.

I have fun hiking with my family at Chimney Rock State Park.

Country music star Luke Combs was born in North Carolina. NBA **point guard** Chris Paul was also born in North Carolina.

Fun Fact: U.S. senator and author Elizabeth Dole was born in Salisbury, North Carolina.

My favorite beaches are in Surf City.

The U.S. National Whitewater Center is a fun place to watch **kayaking**.

# Glossary

**capital** (cap-ih-tuhl): The city or town where the government of a country, state, or province is located

**dogwood** (dog-wuhd): A type of tree with white flowers

**kayaking** (kie-yak-ing): A watersport that uses a long, narrow boat that is pointed at both ends

**parkway** (park-way): A wide, landscaped highway

**point guard** (poynt gard): A position on a basketball team

**sweet potatoes** (sweet poh-tay-toes): Orange root vegetables

# Index



# About the Author

Christina Earley lives in sunny South Florida with her husband and son. She enjoys traveling around the United States and learning about different historical places. Her hobbies include hiking, yoga, and baking.

Written by: Christina Earley
Designed and Illustrated by: Bobbie Houser
Series Development: James Earley
Proofreader: Melissa Boyce
Educational Consultant: Marie Lemke M.Ed.

Photographs:
Alamy: Niday Picture Library: p. 19
Newscom: Brian Rothmuller/Icon Sportswire DHZ: p. 18 right, 23
Shutterstock: Cvandyke: cover; Gary C. Tognoni: p. 3; Sean Pavone: p. 4, 7, 17; CeGe: p. 5; Volina: p. 6, 22; Brian E Kushner: p. 8; PAUL ATKINSON: p. 9, 22; sky-and-sun: p. 10-11, 23; KarepaStock: p. 11; railway fx: p. 12; Grindstone Media Group: p. 13; anthony heflin: p. 14-15, 23; Jon Bilous: p. 15; Anne Kitzman: p. 16; Debby Wong: p. 18 left; Brooke Becker: p. 20; MattManaged: p. 21, 22

## Crabtree Publishing

crabtreebooks.com 800-387-7650



**Printed in the U.S.A./012023/CG20220815**

**Published in Canada**
**Crabtree Publishing**
616 Welland Avenue
St. Catharines, Ontario
L2M 5V6

**Published in the United States**
**Crabtree Publishing**
347 Fifth Avenue
Suite 1402-145
New York, New York, 10016

**Library and Archives Canada Cataloguing in Publication**
Available at Library and Archives Canada

**Library of Congress Cataloging-in-Publication Data**
Available at the Library of Congress

Hardcover: 978-1-0396-9654-9
Paperback: 978-1-0396-9761-4
Ebook (pdf): 978-1-0396-9975-5
Epub: 978-1-0396-9868-0